Also by
Ellen Marie Metrick

Books:
Poetisattva
Tonics for Disembodiment

Broadsides:
Squatters' Bill of Rights
After Summer Dust and Shimmer
Happily Ever After

"These are daring poems, poems that take equal delight in wrapping themselves in veils and letting all the masks drop. How willing are we to see the world as it is? To see ourselves as we are? Ellen Marie Metrick, with language both playful and cutting, leads us to our own wells where we can almost glimpse our source."

—Rosemerry Wahtola Trommer, *The Miracle Already Happening*

"There is a trembling and humility in Ellen's poetry that overwhelms me. Her connection to self never suffocates her deeper experience of family and nature."

—Kit Hedman

"Come in. Come into this book. Ellen Metrick's voice is vibrantly present on every page, inviting us into caves, skies, dreams, and her ongoing conversation with life itself, be it argument or prayer. If you're lucky, this book will find its way into your hands, and into your heart. If you're even luckier, you'll hear Ellen embody these poems aloud when she walks beside a river, or steps up to a microphone. Come in, and stay."

—Barbara Ford, host of Poets and Minstrels on KHEN 106.9 FM Salida, Colo.

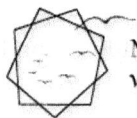

Teasing
out the
Divine

Teasing
out the
Divine

Ellen Marie Metrick

Teasing out the Divine
Copyright ©2012 Ellen Marie Metrick

ISBN: 978-0-9839935-8-2
Publisher: Mercury HeartLink
Printed in the United States of America

Cover art "Night," pastel by Cynthia Sampson
www.zebrajazzstudio.com, tel. 970-865-2383

Back cover photo and interior portrait photo by Kit Hedman
www.hedmanphoto.com

Permission is granted to educators to create copies of individual poems for classroom or workshop assignments.

Contact Ellen Metrick at metricke@gmail.com

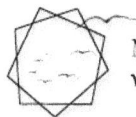

Mercury HeartLink
www.heartlink.com

Thanks to Sue Scavo and Art Goodtimes for saying and hearing, respectively, the title of this collection. Thanks also to Sue for her midwifery, helping to bring dreams into the light, and to the North of Eden community. Thanks to Karen Chamberlain's lasting, loving influence, and to the folks who created and attended her memorial poetry festival in Carbondale, where this book was conceived. Thanks to my readers; Rosemerry Wahtola Trommer, Art Goodtimes, Barbara Ford, Kit Hedman, Amy Irvine McHarg, Sue Scavo, and Shelly Bolus, and to my poetic tribe, scattered though it is. And to the San Miguel County Commissioners for honoring me in April 2011 with the San Miguel County Poet Laureate position.

And thanks to my daughter, for joining me, and to my husband, for supporting me, even though poetry to him is like golf to me; may we both continue to allow space for that which we may never understand. Finally, and forever, thanks to the land that holds us and feeds us.

Some of the poems in this book have appeared in: DeLuge Literary and Arts Journal (www.northofeden.com), Pilgrimage Magazine, Telluride Magazine, Mountain Gazette, The Watch Newspaper, and in the air when they were certain no one was looking.

Contents

THE WORK:

DRAWING WATER

SOURCE

ABOUT THE AUTHOR

To you, dear reader; to you who choose to live,
and to you who have forgotten choice, and to all
who share the journey (you know who you are).

⚘

"It is better to be passionate than to be tolerant at the expense of one's soul." –Freya Stark

"We must be willing to get rid of the life we've planned, so as to have the life that is waiting for us." –Joseph Campbell

"I dream, therefore I exist." –August Strindberg

ALL ALONG

"This earth I have not loved / will hold me."
–David Whyte

This Way In

"I ... am stucco'd with quadrupeds and birds all over."
—Walt Whitman

It must have taken
        a long time.
The grief
a river
        melting slowly at first
                on damp cave walls,
earthmilk dripping from stone.
That slow,
noticed only as scratches
took form; a catalog
        of shapes, a prehistoric
        shopping list, a lithic
        mourning, an invitation
                to our future.

Teasing out the Divine   3

First Day: Chronos

Oh, you're a cold one,
leaving us all alone.
You never stay
unless we play—
don't stick around
when we're sick—
just fly on past
when we wake
with misery's plate
empty before us.

You come and dine,
bring the wine and
chocolate cake,
but skip along
when the bitters
are too strong.

I lie in bed
and you're out there
in a red hat and mittens
swinging from the stars.

I haven't invited you here
in months. I've been
working, in fact,
on a stunt
to avoid you
all together.

FEELING

"A bird in hand is better than three in the wood"

"It's a waste of time," she says. Some small wing
folds in as it always has.

That cottonwood tree—thick-waisted and gnarled—
spreads wide its arms, though it's guarded
by barbed wire, cattails, swampy pond, and I want
to wrap my small arms around its girth.

"A waste of time" echoes in my bones.
Move on. Ride edges. Skim surface. Soar
above. Glove the hand that would touch
rough, deep-grooved bark. Boot the foot
that would smush through muck-sucking slosh.
Glass the eye that would squint
sun glare on still-green leaves.

Fold the wing that would soar home to
nest and brood, preen and feed this hatch.

HELP

Is a call
I don't know how
or when,
where or why
to make.

What color
texture
scent or taste
your voice has
is not known to me,
and I'm not sure how to sense
your particular existence.

What I do know:
the rev of a diesel engine;
walking through days
on my hands
like a maimed superhero;
jumping from cliffs
just to prove I can.

In this, it's easy to forget
that you're there, waiting
in the redrock canyon
for me, your best
earth-brown donned
in my favor.

This, I know.
And the ringing in my ears
is a vigil of lies;
things that bump
all night and day,
knocking me senseless
to your presence. I know
these so well,
I loathe to leave them
in this dark crack in sandstone,
this altar to autumn
and leaving, where I pray
for new beginnings,
a sense of you.

WE ALL DO IT

> *"Why would I want to live and build inside of a cave?"*
> –Mesa Verde National Park ranger, to tour group at Cliff
> Palace.

Before the Puebloans built in these caves, Basketmakers
lived in pit houses, up on the mesa, where they were
warm in winter, cool in summer skin-searing heat.

Much later, Navajo workers, hired by Anglos
to dig pots and bones, called the cave dwellers
by their own name: Anasazi—enemy ancestor.

Who feared them then? And why,
as the ranger asked, on our tour of Mesa Verde, why
did they build here, down these cliffs, in caves?

The first thought, first answer, is for protection.
From enemies, from animals, from weather.
None of us says how cool it might be in summer;
how the food up in the back is safe from rats;
how the wall makes buildings stable;
how the acoustics allow us to speak in whispers
and be heard at distance; how the heat caught is kept,
and how rain and snowmelt seep down through sandstone
to this shale where pools catch the gleaming treasure,
hold it near the homes.

Much later, someone suggests

that building down here leaves more arable land up top.
Not one of us says those things immediately.

We think of safety first, of how we can protect
ourselves from outsiders, from what we don't know
and can only name as enemy, even if ancestor.

While I Am Not Imelda Marcos

There are many times I've wished
for your shoes; your colors, styles, some
high, some flat. I especially loved
the orange wool ones, and the clogs,
those sensible, general-use, go-with-everything
chestnut leather. Some, I could never imagine
fitting me, though I tried, and wanted
to think I could wear them. It's the ones
you wear today that I most envy, though.
Rock-climbing shoes, tied with long,
yolk-yellow laces. They are sticky-soled,
the soft leather purple and green.

Well, I know you're brave. I know
these shoes are made for adventure, for dancing
on heights and smearing risky moves
when the rock face is sheer. I know
they're made for walking through doors in high cliffs,
made for leaping where none could see
a route before—before the moon set as it did

early this morning, tethered to storm, to winds
and coming lash of rain. And still, moon sent
her cool, cyclical light through each break
in today's grey sky.

Absolutely

My name is not, you know; it is,
and I don't know
who I am
if I is
an am
anymore than you
are not me, he, it;
sit for this, cause ain't shit
you, she, it can do;
crawl, hover, deliver brother to sky hovel, shovel
that coal cause its gonna get colder if you don't
come in here with us where it's warm.

DODECAHEDROPUS

Because eight just isn't enough,
I'm a dodecahedropus tonight.

Eight arms is not enough to grab
what I need, to hold close

the love I seek, to wrap up
the one whose sleek streak

heartline chases mine through
the maze while I run, sword in hand,

seeking the head to cut off,
the monster to slay.

No. Slowed by twelve arms,
I will wait. Waiting
or stumbling towards him
is all that's left to do.

HUNGER

The sky has come to rest in our swale.
On the first day, little girls stripped,
then squealing, jumped into its cold. Today,
just below this red house, clouds float
with the mallard pair. Swallows dip
through blue and grey changes, framed
by fallen thatch where green grows,
weaving through. When the wind blows,
as it does through May, the sky ripples to white chop
and bright red wings of blackbirds flash
from swaying cattail tops. All winter, it was
a brown hole where we found tracks
of wandering fox, coyote, bird, deer.
Now, wakes of aimless ducks
disappear into sky's wide capture
where eyes rest and wings stretch
in answer to frogsong and mysterious cries
in late darkness, as if the denizens of night sky
have come out to play, inviting sleepers
to strip and jump
into spring stars ... for even the gods
desire Earth's children.

FULL CUP

Thinking:
Not good.
Feeling?
Good.
$137.22:
Not good.
Sigh.
In your words,
I feel wanted.
Presence, like
wine,
spills.
Oh, dear.
You, again.

AMEN

There are certain things that must happen
before a poem is born. First, there must be
silence. In the woods, or in the house, I must
be alone. Second, there must be time. A lot
of it. Third, there must be a full moon, in
my heart or in the sky, by which to write,
and the perfectly flowing pen, and just
the right weight and heft of paper.
Lastly, if any one of these rules becomes
an excuse, if it stops me from writing,
as they all have, I now realize, for the past
seven years, nine months, 18 days, 6 hours
and 13 minutes, then it is very likely time
for new rules.

INVITATION

Have you heard
of Isis and Osiris?
Of He and She?
Of One? Of We?
Oh, Brother of flesh and blood;
Sister of drought and flood;
Lovers from other lives,
in this life I want to mix
our spit with soil,
trade our skins for sun,
spin our nerves from chi-touch—
that wild slipping of geese,
that please-oh-please
of do-it-again pleasure.

Oh, Man who is the Woman
to touch my Man;
Woman who hides in the Man
who is Me—Dance! Dance!
Dance the wild word-wind
of one-lettered measure.

The mule of my intellect
lies down at your feet,
sighing its desire to be loved
like this, between the howl
and whisper of birth and death,
wended and blending

into the sacred treasure
of stones, and leaves, and oceans.

Oh, seed of my soul,
kiss the lizard! Climb
the ridge! Slide through
the gates into the glacier
lake of life! Kundalini

is tonguing the earth
for your scent, rising
to meet you halfway
between nerves
and ether.

WITH OR WITHOUT YOU

This is the fear; sit with him,
Here. Nothing you must do, you say
again, to yourself. Nothing. Simple,
but here you go, up and dusting,
arranging knick-knacks above
this too-narrow-for-two bed, while he
stands there, just inside the door.
He's closed it, and now waits,
hat in hand, for you
to turn.

You suspect he could wait all day.
He would, while you could
take a toothbrush, a lifetime
to clean this tiny apartment.

There is something he wants you to do.
That's what he said last time you met,
when he held your face in his hands
like a father. You remember that fierce
tenderness like lightning and rain.

Your vision blurs, you grip the gathered
feathers, and continue dusting, while your heart
turns towards the door without you.

THE WORK:
DRAWING WATER

*"It is by going down into the abyss that we recover the treasures
of life. Where you stumble, there lies your treasure."*
–Joseph Campbell

Compass Point

Is this my needle, my North;
this sorrow by birth, the worth
of my howl, my how? Only now,
as the trail peaks mountain,
do I find mind giving way
to sky, hawks hooking way
from why. Oh, High Stones;
oh, Cairn of My Woe, this
burrow, this hoed row rolls me
undertow. Only a bat
could find me now. I am
naught but sound, waving
this exquisite existence,
this pittance, a single glitter
in sky's wide skirt.

Back to Narnia

"Indeed, don't try to get there at all."
–Professor Digory Kirke

There is not a thing you can do. It's not like that.
Try as you may, the only way in is through
the golden keyhole of each day as it is,
the rough touch of applewood gleam
through time's dust-caught air. It's not
the fruit every day; sometimes
a tree has to grow, bend in hail and
wind—blister, even. Sometimes this fruit
has to be picked and eaten, this seed
thrown down and somehow be sown
by bootstep or hoe. And sometimes,
the only thing you can do
is borrow a fur coat,
follow lightgleam seen through scratching branches,
and leave your known world behind.

If You're Going, Go All the Way

You're looking
for the path, the way, the teacher
to take you There.
You tell yourself,
"All roads.
All roads lead There."
Yet you keep reading, listening, seeking.

And then, one day,
resting in shade
beside the road,
urging yourself
in the same old way
to go on,
you tell yourself,
"It's the only way,"
while you are struck dizzy
with thirst, heat, grit.

On that day, the notion strikes you—
not just a bright bulb
of thought,
but a shiver,
a mountain river,
a cool runnel
down sternum bone, and
your shoulders drop
from around your ears.
Your hands open.

It's as if a large cat
has just lain down
in the cradle of your pelvis,
all purr and heat.

It's like that.
And you know
this road,
this day,
this moment
with its heat and sting and sharp blades—
this is your way.
It has been.
It will be.
And there's not a damn thing
you can do about it.

CROSSROADS

Hills green and open-ended
roll and rise in dawn's kaleidoscope.
Crested Butte peak births
the yellow mother morning bird,
weaving sky to soil, to blue, to green,
to you, to me. Weaving in trickster's
black beginning blessing. Weaving
honey gold shadow and light
over this hilltop, an offering
of early purple blossom, mirror
dandelion and yarrow.

Open the red door
in the center of breath; inhale
new heat in the solar plexus.

It is clear now, how the snake
lays her egg beneath our skin.
To shed the winter layer,
we open and slide through
this thin crack of fear.

What I've tried to say
rests in evening's belly,
carried by the scent
of snake at the edge
of the well. It thrives
in the space between
brain and heart and body,

beginning each dawn
at this crossroads
between prison and place,
and ending each day
in the candid resolve
of raven-wing iridescent dusk.

FISHING
for the kids at WSCF summer camp, 2006

Whose idea was this, anyway? I ask,
wishing it had not been mine. I apologize
to each beady black eye, "Oops, sorry," as I
disentangle claws and tails from the net.

The kids squeal, I got one! Look out!
Comin' through! Somebody bring
a net! Aww, he got off! Is this one
too small? I'm bringing Blue Lips
home!

By the time we reach camp, twelve
crawdads have been claimed and named:
Big Daddy, Squelch, Captain Busy.
Two boys toss the rest into
boiling water. We all eat while
the live pets crawl across the table,
or watch from pans of cold water, and

I wonder at the way we all love some
and eat the others, and at the excitement
of drawing them up and out
of the water, dripping with silver
and lakeweed, claws flailing in the air
for a grip at something familiar, tails

flashing as they are grabbed
by our own pincers behind their front

pinching legs, and placed in a bucket
of crowded water, where it is
all clasp and antennae test, seeking
free space—all of us fishing
for a way out of the shallow bucket.

Not How I Imagined

This is not how I imagined it. No steaming
cup of tea or window view; no swelling crescendo
of strings, blaze of dawn, or red carpet to the muse's
temple.
It's not amusing. The way I finally come to the page—late,
still in pajamas, hair tousled, at 11:37 a.m., to write
my aubade—is not how I imagined it would be.

The wind is furious, flinging steel dog bowls clanging
across the concrete porch. I sit sideways, hunched
in my posture-correct desk chair, notebook propped
on one knee, eyes brimming, hole widening in my chest,
breath ragged at the edges of an ancient knife wound, a
knot
swelling beneath the left shoulder blade. And the phone
rings.

Even though I just, finally, forced myself to sit. Still. I
answer.
While I'm on the house phone, the cell phone rings. And
I'm deep
into e-mailing follow-ups to the calls before I realize,

I've abandoned a poem.

It waits, but I've left it completely. This is not how I
imagined
I would write today. It is a fight. I try to let Mary Oliver's
advice

inhabit my blood, but—I worry about getting it right. I want
to be good, and the only soft animal in my body today
is a skittering squirrel scratching Morse code in my skull
stippling an S.O.S. of what's next and next and next and
today did not yank me through the door of the lover's
house.

I know it is always open. I know that if I want it, it's up to me
to step into the opening—now, and after the phone rings, and even
in the center of the squirrel cage—but today, I can't find the lee or the lean
of this electric wind. I am afraid to step into the light and swirl of this new love.

Autumn Song

Just falling; into
soil, ground, humus, skeleton
left above surface, all green
gone to rot, to roll away
in autumn wind.

Dive down, out of the air, into
snake den, into roil of slither, skin
to skin, now, we sleep, breathe
stony air below frost line. We
keep warm wrapped together, until
creep-forth time in warming

season, until we unroll, unwrap, go
our separate ways for heat. Then,
we shed our skins alone, in the company
of sun, stone, grass to hide this
vulnerable body when we can't see,
can't hear; when the skin is a muffle
around the head, like going down
into the soil again. Going down,

over and over as we grow, shed,
come alive, die, bring forth our bodies
from old, from winter, from soil,
from humus, to creep and crawl, to slither
soft through season and slough.

Not up to Us

"How could I have lived so long / If I had not known that day /
Was bound to come in the end?"
—Eiléan Ní Chuilleanáin

We build our castles in the grand style, with
manicured gardens and imagined moats
from inside our dark homes. We tell ourselves
we will find day when we find the way out.
In that imagined light, we see how tall we'll sit
on our glowing steeds, how our armor
will glint and shine after stooping,
crouching with hardscrabble arachnids,
ears punched with the crunch and stutter
of this web, sound of doubt strangling desire.

What if we knew what the fishermen know—
that the castles are bait; that caught fish
will be head-struck, gutted,
eaten around the fire at dark.

What if this seaweed forest
is just where we live, a tunnel
in the lava flow, and in the end
it is not a dangling salmon egg
but the current itself—even weeds
bow to its power—the current
that will one day pull us
from under-boulder dark
into sun-glittered stream.

EVER WONDER HOW

Under the wound is wonder,
is a wound-door, is light
wound around bone.

Each wound is a door, opens
on light, lets in the red bird,
remembered flight

screaming for a link, a lit line
from soul to sun,
from separation to repatriation.

To incise opens desire, where
bloodflower blooms
from passion's bud,

scents this grey stone of existence
with wonder, as water sends
flat lichen onto tiptoe tendrils
in bright orange swells of praise.

STONE'S THROW
an homage to rocks

Since, as far as all our intelligence knows,
you don't move of your own volition,
but use our hands, feet, backs,
forklifts to go, and since you rely also
on the gravity of freeze and thaw and
wind and rain, and because at sunrise
and sunset you soften like soulshine,

I would offer you anything. Even this truck,
my way of moving through the world,
(because I have already given you,
time and again, my shins and knees,
my elbows, and head).

Today, as I drive over this winding pass,
I also give you also my patience
as I watch for falling rock. I give you
my surprise at how more often than not
you land—not on my truck,
not under my wheels—at the edge
of each lane. You land and roll away.

I can't discount the possibility
that this was done by choice.

SIGNS OF THE TIMES

Watch for Rocks Next 45 Miles,
sign says. Sign says, Tractor Crossing.
Deer Next 13 Miles. No Parking.

It's dark, and the road tonight
is long. Signs aren't helping. What
did help was your headlights
opening the canyon before mine,
your taillights before me in the swirl
of blowing snow. But that was

last night. Tonight, I am alone
in the dark again, stone pressing
from high cliffs, river rumbling
to the left. To relax, I remind myself

every moment is a poem.
Gas, Food, Lodging Next Right;
50 MPH Curve; Bridges May Be Icy.
I miss the turnoff, come back around
to try again. There are no signs
for what I'm about to do, though

in theory, it's not difficult:
Just step out into air so thin
it slices old skin
right off.

COSMOLOGICALLY SPEAKING
for Star-Man Danny

It's no dis-aster; the stars have everything
to do with this. It's not about explosions
any longer. It is about expansion, proximities,
red shift, and deep field images.
It's about imaginary lines flying
from each person on this shining Earth,
meeting out near Andromeda somewhere,
a present that's long past.

Because objects seem to change direction
based on where we stand,
it's about laws of gravity, by God,
'cause something's gotta keep us
from going for every star at once.

Possibility is a delicious place to visit,
but when I lived there, I had no feet.
I still want all my windows open
to the sweep of night, where
the ancient fires find us now.

Those lives lived may be alive yet,
and we can name them, count the light years,
but we can't buy their sparkle,
because brightness follows the law
of inverse squares and it's the atmosphere
Here
that makes them shimmer.

Our North Star may not be the brightest one;
it takes some work to find it, after all, to follow it
when we're lost, but even apple seeds
are guarded by stars.

Just gazing at Alpha, Beta Centauri, the Southern
Cross and backbone of the universe
can make at least one man happy, and I remember
a lifetime ago, in the Pacific,
tracing the way of souls, finding center, finding peace
while I balanced on rocks beside sea chop and windspray.

The stars are all this, and once you see
the magic dragon, whipping his tail across the night,
you'll never lose him. So learn these stories,
my dears, because
one hundred million years
is a short life
for a star.

Midnight

The cows are crazy. It's weaning time.
A night of wails, cows calling, everyone

unhappy. Our human children
tell us, I miss you more than ever.

Color is leaving Earth, leaves already gone,
garden skeletons abound.

Persephone has picked her flower.
Demeter shakes out her white cape.

It will be months before
the pomegranate is bitten.

The yearning is only just begun.

THE NEXT STEP

Does it occur to her (not quite a sledgehammer),
as she stands in the night breeze,
hearing grasses shift in their beds, the fawn buzzing
to its mother, the deer munching beyond the fence
(a sound any grazing animal might make: comfort)...
does she wonder what he wants? Or is she
thinking only of her escape route?
Does she not know that his black bull
comes only when there is reason?
He hungers for her fear. She is listening.
Listening as we do, waking from a scary dream,
laying in bed as still as stones in winter lay,
listening with every pore, every hair,
the body an ear curled around darkness,
listening as perhaps Christ did, that first night,
hoping for God to speak. Does she wonder,
will there be a bridge in the darkness?
Or just a hole?

MAKERS OF HEAVEN AND EARTH
for G, once, and always, with humility and gratitude.
I am forever bowing.

Poem—from Greek poein, *to make*

I met my muse today.
I met my muse today, oh, boy;
a café latte samba beat body rhythm,
a rockslide roll in grass, a shakewater
heat wave in the metered
sass and surge of savory verse, urging
breath to turn and flare and fire.

But, oh, that love could be
so exclusively easy, so mono-tuned
uni-directional. What can I do?
I love in 24-track, surround sound stereo!
I love you, and I love you, and I love you,
and you, and you! Hey, we're all
talkin' love. Don't have to get
in bed, do it from across the room
at 50 paces, 'cause

it's all in the eyes, darling,
and I can see yours turned,
but not blind, behind the lines
the poet's drawn. It's all in the tongue,
honey, where voice
runs through brain's boulder field,

weathering granite, grinding
sand dunes for a loose journey.
It's all in the hands, love, and
we don't even have to touch;

I can see by your spread
how you make love to pen, paper
your pathway to ecstatic states.
Blame no poet for despair! The air's
too thin up here for that! Make way
for the flare and unfurl of prayer flags!
We're all each other's gurus
and devotees on this mountaintop.

Open the gates, enter Word, O bards
of beat and breath. The flurry of fingers
on drum or live skin matters not, 'cause
it's all in the heart, love,
and the only forever
exists in the ribs' rise and fall, the call
of journey-road, the walls we raze.

Burn the condos! Ignite the contracts!
Flame into town and turn your heart
on the spit of love. Eat
charred risk, sniff
jasmine on the rising wind,
and make merry! Make!

Make love! Be the makers you are,
the poets of heaven and earth. Be

the lovers, the lost ones, the Buddha,
the birds. Be

the Word

and make merry. Make life. Make
the grade, make a run for it, make out,
but don't just make do. Make it up
as you go along. Make your bed, don't
sleep the night away; make arrangements,
make a plan. Make way for ducklings.
Make the ridge by dawn. Make up
your mind! Make the leap, Darling;

I can make it through life
without a wedding day, but I can't
make a sound
without you.

Oh, muse,
you groove me! Word brothers,
word sisters, makers of beat,
pound your pace and rhythm,
sound my skin
deep.

Oh, muse of musk and neck-to-neck,
oh, muse of waning moon, you fill
my womb with word-seeds, suns
of a blood-red belly-gram. Let's
eddy out

and swirl again, soon, friends,
in this current of shoulder-blade breath
where the pages
are always
turning.

TONICS FOR DISEMBODIMENT

I. Stars

Unhitch that Safe-way trailer
from your semi-truck; leave it
by the side of the road.
Somebody else will need it,
and besides, it's empty;
it has been
for a long time.

II. Moon

Canyon walls vibrate
with bat calls. Rattlesnakes
lie spiraled beneath
cooling boulders.
Earth's spin
reveals celestial bodies.
This is not the time
for sleep; we have owl's
vision when we keep
our eyes open.

III. Sun

It always comes to this;
green grass bending
toward autumn when
a friend you thought
you'd never see again
calls, says she's in town.

Don't sweep the floor!
Trim basil, slice
warm bread,
pour the wine!

IV. Dance

I'm done with battle words.
I'm not fighting
colds or flu anymore,
not fighting you.

Let's tangle our limbs
in samba tango groove
or slow waltz.

When it snows, build
a snowman—don't wait
for some god to appear!
Go find a rainstorm
and sing that song.

Rainy Season

"*I am not done with my changes.*"
—Stanley Kuntiz

Some days, I imagine
I am water. Not water
lolling in a bath or basin
of sandstone; not rimmed
with seasonal high marks,
but flowing—flotsaming and
jettisoning over boulders,
around bends, between
black granite arching closed
overhead.

Where once I was thin
and lithe, I am now all
bellow and brace, the sky
all spurls of spume fuming,
funneling all my focus
into flowing.

Holding
no roots,
taking
no breaks,
eddying out
for no one,
but flying

in my own
falling time,

while the trees
and the fish
accept my wet kisses,
like mothers
who turn their cheeks
gleefully
towards the mouths
of happy-tongued children.

Source

"This is the secret of the pomegranate—that the blood tears become the chalice that is one's very own soul to be filled with Divine love."
−The Deep Well Tapes: The Secret of the Pomegranate,
Marc Bregman with Sue Scavo

TODAY, THE MEADOWLARKS
for Japan, in spring

Imagine:
      You wake up
   and the whole sky is
         blown open.
   The roof, gone.
         You had plans today.
   But there goes the car
         on a wave of
   Someone Else's plans, and now—
         now, the whole house is moving
around you.
   Nothing any longer
   stands still
         except you.
         You, for this moment
            have your feet planted
         in full meeting with
the concrete earth—
   this earth
         that so far
has been here every day
         in your waking, and in
         your sleep.

And now,
imagine that
this end, this absolute destruction
decimation disheveled black sky water dawn,

imagine that this is you
        waking up
        and getting a second
        chance.
            In fact, imagine everyone around you
receiving the same gift, a second chance,
at the same time,
waking up at last.
    What will all of you
    do
    with this gift?

Some, even today, as grim and gristled and splintered as it is,
some will keep their eyes shut tight
and complain
about the collapsed peaks, the houses washed out to sea,
the plans.
But you—
    and even some of those
close to you,
    and some
        you will never know—
you and they
are beyond sleep.
As hard as it is
    to walk when the earth
    is all buckle and bow beneath you,
the sky blowing above and around ...
as heartbreaking
    to see the sleepwalkers
falling into the caverns

welcoming them into
    the closing earth ...
as blinded as you are
    by the tears
            washing out the grit of regrets,
you are simply done
    with once upon,
and are Here.
You, and the others, are here
opening your arms,
welcoming and holding the found
children,
listening for the songs
            that will lead you into spring,
            as tonight, below my house, in the south pasture,
            the meadowlarks
            are announcing their renewed presence
            in a multitude of tremors.

BOULDER FIELD ZEN

Crossing the loose tongues of Lone Cone's rock glacier
—it's like learning again to bike downhill
on a single-track, rock-stubbed, hard-pack
winding trail complete with stumps
and downed trees.

I was 20, then, a couple of Fat Tires
in the blood to take my mind off fear.
It took a certain tenuous momentum,
and my friend behind me yelling, let go!
Just let go of the brakes! Let go!

And I did. After weeks of crashing,
bumbling, bumping, I let go and flew,
with a sudden ease and nimbleness
I'd envied in others. I flew down Horse Gulch
yawping and whooping with wind yanking my hair
into a banner of freedom unfurling behind me.

And I remember it today, 23 years later,
stippling across this rock-filled cirque called
Devil's Chair. I am goat or mountain sheep,
following feet to find rocktopple drumroll-
clatter clinkpop, jumping from tottering talus
platter to boulder to jumble of rock, knowing
it'll move, and moving right along with it, traveling
at the speed of tipping. Trusting foot, not eye,

now, and remembering, again, how to play pretend.
Today, I am alpine goat, feeling myself lift
out of mind and into mountain.

EQUAL

Guilt rides me like a whipping jockey,
busy drives me; I am a cart horse
with my head bent, a dervish
in red shoes. I have no map
for tomorrow and that
fuels panic.

I stop at a park bench where
a man and a women sit. They hold
light in their teeth. I ask directions.
"Oh, but we're going with you.
Didn't you know?"

It is spring today;
light and dark meeting to dance.
I balance between
equal to the task when I remember
to hold their outstretched hands.

VISIBLE

I see you, yes—you are
the impossible route
up granite, seen only
one move at a time,
found more by fingertip
than eye.

I see you, yes—you are
the line through trees
in deep powder, seen
then lost, visible
to knees and feet, a sense
of give and take
in muscles' break and bend.

I see you. Yes, I see; you are
the smooth tongue of water
mid-river, where sky's blue reflection
leads the way through
white churn and rapid chop,
where the downstream
current line is fine, and
where a single oar-dip
is the difference
between slide
and flip.

No Regrets

Aspens shimmer gold shaking
2,000 feet below our careful toes
where graupel pelts granite talus,
surrounds us with the sound
of bamboo wind chimes, stops
us in our descent just to listen.

The snow-hail stings our faces
and we move, blizzard blind. Scent
of struck flint is all that's missing,
I think, as I step and pencil a windchime
haiku. And then, a tingling, my neck
prickling, and static fills my ears
as though my mp3 lost the radio station
but I wear no earbuds, I realize, as I reach
to remove them. And then, the missing
scent, burning ozone, reaches my nose
and I holler back to Ang, GET DOWN!

I laugh now. She yelled, What? through
the wind and I had to repeat, already 20 feet
below her and the exposed ridge, GET DOWN,
and through the hiss of storm I heard
her, OH! And we're off the stable spine of table rock,
down into loose scree and slush, a scramble
in a slow-mo scuttle over scaping sleet-slick
stone with lightning crackling the charged air—
the only sound other than thunder and the pelt
pock of pellet snow on rock, now

deep in slush, charming chime hidden
in scary slipcover of sliding stone—that
schuss sound we don't want to hear, carrying
our footsteps down the steep slope in uncontrolled
tumble-roll.

And then, we're down. Trees.
We're moving steady, again, after slips and slides
and almost-tumbles. We dodge into snow-white
woods scented with wet, the prick pine needles
dry underfoot, welcomes us. We can see
a dark swirl of storm rounding the peak again
with lit fingers, and we laugh, a muffled sound
in wet trees. Feeling safe, now, we say
both at the same time,
I wouldn't trade that descent
for anything.

FIRE MEN

*for the Japanese workers who went in to clean up the Fukushima
reactor site*

This morning, the moon
spun down in a bank of rusted clouds,
itself orangey brown as horizon hid glow.

The cloud of sickness must be here by now.
It cannot be seen like flies or locusts or crows;
its blackness is deeper than those,

eating a body away from the inside.
Those people at the center—
Kamikaze, gods of wind, flying in

to rescue death himself from
his own slow but certain hand—
they will have time to say farewell, though

by then, none will go near their heat,
clicking like a century of cicadas
crouching in tree crooks at dusk,
robbing the night herself of sleep.

Meadowlarks at Midnight

They call out—lovers, rivals,
dreamers—sounding a clear liquid light
through deep dark. They circle my sleep like

wing beats of lost kin. Mornings
find them carrying sunlight
to each fencepost, breastbones

resonating memory.
All day they translate
a forgotten journey, as if

pinfeathers could sprout
from my eyelids—
as if my fingers were

small flames, lit wicks pricking
deep-cave dark.

The Gate is Open

The cave entrance
is pitch and yaw at your back. For decades
you've wanted this moment, this way out,
but now the red cord you dropped
in excitement only moments ago, in celebrating
the end of this life, is bright in the greening grass.

It is a snake wrapped around your warm ankle,
a tendril of jasmine vine vying with the vista
for your attention.

The suitcase at your side
has been packed for years, waiting
in the back of the closet for this day.

This story you've told to keep yourself here
is already dissolving, early snow in autumn sun, sending
muddy waters to grass of here, where your life
has been waiting all along.

HOME
for the kids at WSCF summer camp, 2006

> *"stay together / learn the flowers / go light"*
> —Gary Snyder

> *"... in their innocence and trusting, they will teach us to be free"*
> —John Denver

They kept saying, I hope no one comes,
not ever! We'll sleep here!

They smeared dandelions on each other, burning
with summer's rich colors. They giggled,
squealed, slipped down the mud banks
of the cold beaver pond, screaming.

They popped the heads off flowers, chanting an old song.
Skipped rocks, holding an older silence. Teamed up to haul
boulders
to the river's edge; push, and plop-splash.

They whittled sticks. Caught frogs, mayflies,
spiders, centipedes, water skippers and boatmen.
They waded, laughed, ran, flung moss and mud and grass.

As Lone Cone peak rolled toward the sun
and shadows spread across the meadow,
they sat in the shade and drew pictures,
wrote stories, stared at the water
with liquid eyes. They smacked mosquitoes

and watched a couple of red-shafted flickers
flit in and out of their nesting hole
high in a standing dead aspen.

When it was time to leave, and the key
broke off in the van door lock, they just kept saying,

I hope no one comes, not ever! We'll sleep
just fine here. We'll stay close together.

What There Is to Remember

If you had been there, you would have seen
two ravens perched on the nearest telephone pole.

These were not metaphorical ravens, and the pole
was wooden, black with creosote, pungent in the heat.

This is not some urban telephone pole. It is in a pasture,
near what we here call the highway, which is really

a two-lane blacktop that goes west, and east,
stretching between peaks and desert. Really,

it is the way out, and in; the way through
weeping canyons and Paradox. It is the way

to Bedrock, salt, sorrow, old Ute and Navajo trails,
and pictures that talk. But bring your eyes away

from that distance. Center is this high mesa, circled
by mountains, hazy with distance. Come back

to these two ravens. I think they are kissing, or one is
feeding the other, and the sound they are making—

if you listen, hear the mid-range gurgle? Almost,
yes, it is laughter, I'm sure. And if you keep listening,

eyes on those two ravens, you can hear, through
the wind, the grasses; their dry instruments, an orchestra

of sighs. There, too, hear the cricket, mid-day, one
continuous yearning, or perhaps he is laughing, too.

Right now there are no cars on the blacktop.
Wind, laughter, sighs. And, look—these grasses

leaning together: green, yellow, orange, brown,
and red, purple—only blue is missing, as if the sky

has soaked it all up for itself. And the raven's wings
steal some blue from that sky. Keep standing here,

notice how the wind feels on your cheek. It is not cold.
Not hot. September at 7,000'. Need I say more? Feel

your t-shirt ripple across your belly, the cuffs of your pants
tapping your ankles, ears hollowed out by this wind, hair

pulled back in a bandana so it doesn't whip the eyes. Why
am I telling you all of this? I tell you because this moment,

standing beneath chuckling, inside the whispering, near
the yearning, I tell you: It is not those ravens, nor the dog

sitting next to us, nor the wind itself; it is not the absence
of vehicles, nor the smell of the decaying cat in the next

pasture, nor the dry dust in the nostrils; it is not the hot
sun on your cheek. It is none of these things. It is

all of them. They are all settling somewhere deep
in the belly, in my knees and footpads, in my buttocks

and softening shoulders, in this light in my eyes, all
settling so that suddenly I have neither skin nor eye.

I have neither ear nor nose. I am and I am not
this moment, the mountain, the bending grass,

the river I can't see, and scrub oak I can see, leaving
green for rust, and must I tell you? I am and I am not here,

I feel you being and not being. Skin sloughing,
we become the dust underfoot, the blue wing

of reflection, the song of grasses remembering green.

HALF-GONE

The girl with one eye sees half
inside, misses things most see,
sees what many don't. Behind
closed-lid darkness breathes
sorrow. Rivers run
backward, underground, near images
pecked into skull walls where beings
slide from solid stone. She needs
no one. She knows alone like her own
skin, slips like a sown seed
into her own being, light shining
from starholes
beak-pecked into sky
skull.

Sound of Two Hands Catching

The bat flutters
    from the dry mouth of her cave
    seeing a certain angle
of sound,
    and today
        I was your dinner.
  I felt your sonar
      bounce
       so that suddenly I was known
to myself
    as edible.

AFTER SUMMER DUST AND SHIMMER

Oh, let me be roasted
'til the sweet ting of these crimson bells
rings in my bones, 'til blood runs
bright as this slick warm flesh
slipped from its charred skin.

Oh, that I could be seared
'til tight flesh gives way beneath
tongue's wet, bursts into thrust of
caramelized sun on gums and
teeth, sings in the fecund language
only abundance speaks.

Oh, to be plucked
from this still-green skeleton
of late summer, palmed
like warm plum tomatoes, popped
in the mouth like these
firm cherry buttons bursting.

Oh, I could thrive here
in this cliff-steeped river loam heat
where hearts fly on swallow-sharp
wings. Right now, this season is our art,
hearts in full fledge, soaring with
summer's abundance.

Our art is season; plant, hoe, pluck, can, eat, sleep.

Autumn is as close as the cold woodstove,
　　forgotten in plain view since thaw,
　　　　just as all too often I forget you.

　　　　Come, let us lie down
in this roasting pan, let the flames change
　　　　bitter flesh to sweet succulence.

Trinity

a take on Crow Mother, Her Eyes, Her Eggs
—a painting by Meinrad Craighead

Wrapped to the breast
  in a python's grip,
   birthed in the backseat
        with shredded wings.
Black beak black sky.
  White shocked lightning wrapped
    to cover the head;
don't look too close at me
  it's all dark chasm
    behind my broken shell.
Snake skin slither, that thin
  shiver; recognition rises
    with silver-shake and rattle-hiss.
Eyes on every feather
birth the snake, eat the snake
snake eats you.
Lightning underfoot is a
  static dance
    we do in wooing
      the world we imagine
          wanting,
until the length of it
cracks ribs.
Old crone's bony fingers,

maiden's wings,
mother's prison: This
is the trinity we live,
our feminine existence.

BARBED WIRE

The whip is sharp. It's as if
she put barbs in the tip.
You roll, beg, pounce, dance
on hind legs. You jump
before she speaks,
try and trump
the stinging lash.
She is all wrist, can't
resist crack of air;
fist-first she crows
her existence. Strut
and gleam is her means
to beat survival.
To rival Truth.
Her heat glimmers,
a spell, and you can't see
the well for the water.
Beyond corral and pasture,
trees offer sweet
freedom. The gate
is open. Rise and run.
Do you dare?

HERE IS YES

Yes, who fills this old wooden bowl, oiled
   with years of eating. Yes, where blue

         horizons and lightning meet.
      Yes where the clay remembers waves,

   where there are no doors, no windows, only
   openings in low walls, only woman shapes.

      This is where the boy makes the bear
   who stares, open-mouthed in delight at stars.

      Yes opens her arms here and lives
   with her strong hands and long yellow hair,

         clay still sticking to her bare heels.

THE WOMAN AT THE WELL

A blue scarf, draped; the shine of water
echoing on her face above the well;
she is the pump, the fountain
of tears.

The woman at the well
was a child, once; the sun
in her hair was fire and his eyes
were also wells.
That was how she knew
she had to do something, even as simple
as drawing him a drink of that deep water.

She knew then, he had been there
all along,
though up she had never looked,
up before dipping her jar
into the deep water.

All her life, head down,
scarf wound about head, neck, shoulders,
watching for the stones
that would trip her,
send her jar to the hard ground
in splinters of shining clay.

Now, the hem of her dress
is wet.

Now, he is standing beside her, where
he has always been.
Beside her, as ever, only today
—as she bent, lowering her jar—
today, she looked up.

Ellen Marie Metrick is currently the editor/reporter/ photographer for the usually 8-page Norwood Post, which covers the news of a little town that sits on a high desert mesa at 7,000' between a river canyon and an old volcano, between bedrock and clear, starry skies. She is also partner and mother in a family of three, and aunt, daughter and sister in her larger family.

As San Miguel County Poet Laureate, she asks residents to invite a poet to dinner, and open their homes to the magic of poetry and community. Once a river guide, Ellen is now stage hand and director of children's theater in Norwood at The Livery. She's been teaching children and young adults in one way or another for nearly 30 years, and theater is the most recent passion she shares with them. Ellen is also the curator of the ACE of Norwood Talking Gourd Circle series at The Livery.

In addition to theater and poetry, Ellen's loves are people, story, myth, and a good walk in the woods or a float down a desert river. Her first book, *Poetisattva*, was published in 2000.

Colophon

The typefaces used in this book are California FB (TrueType), Kozuka Gothic Pro (PostScript), and Trajan Pro (PostScript). Book designer Stewart Warren used several Adobe Creative Suite applications including Photoshop and InDesign.

www.ingramcontent.com/pod-product-compliance
Lightning Source LLC
Chambersburg PA
CBHW052057270326
41931CB00012B/2795